More Adult Skills from Lawler Education

KU-494-147

Spelling
More Spelling
Even More Spelling
Cloze
Cloze: Cars and Transport
Vital Phonics 1
Writing and Forming Numbers (Entry Level)
Writing and Forming Letters (Entry Level)
Understanding Maths
Supermarket Maths
Grammar
More Grammar
Menu Maths
Reading Comprehension
More Reading Comprehension
Guided Reading and Writing
Punctuation
Applications and Forms
Family Life
Skills for Life

Many more titles in preparation

Teacher note

This resource covers many of the ideas that a teacher of adult literacy or English for speakers of other languages could use, in order to help their students in developing the ability to hold as conversation. The work in this book will also help students to increase their vocabulary in English and help them in everyday situations at home, work or in the community.

We have included work that is both structured for improved learning as well as being informal at times. The purpose of this work is to help you to help your students become more confident speakers.

Judith Parfitt

Please note that the Smart board files and the audio files for this book are loaded on the disc that comes with the book.

© 2016 Lawler Education
Teachers may copy these pages for use in their own school. Rights are not transferable.

4   © 2016 Lawler Education
      Teachers may copy these pages for use in their own school. Rights are not transferable.

Lawler Education ▶ *Adult Skills*

SKILLS FOR LIFE

Judith Parfitt B.Ed.
Cert.Ed. Adv.Dip. Ed.

526 673 84 X

SKILLS FOR LIFE

Judith Parfitt B.Ed., Cert. Ed., Adv. Dip. Ed.
The author's rights have been asserted.

© 2016 GLMP Ltd All Rights Reserved.

978-1-84285-416-7

Reprinted 2017

Produced and Published by
Lawler Education
Lamorna House
Abergele
LL22 8DD

www.graham-lawler.com

Lawler Education is a division of GLMP Ltd

Copyright Notice
The copyright of this book grants the right for one tutor at one provider site to photocopy the activities. A Multi-User Licence must be purchased for each additional tutor using the same resource at the same site. Additional Multi-User licences can be purchased at any time.
For providers with multiple sites, each site is treated as an independent site and the above paragraph applies.
The ongoing supply of these materials depends on tutors' professional good judgment and compliance with copyright law. This resource is covered by UK and European copyright law, and CLA polices its use.

Image page 34 courtesy of www.public-domain-image.com

Teacher Notes

1 Purpose
The purpose of this unit is to encourage students to form questions, ask questions, listen to answers and ask further questions. We have used this material with small groups, larger groups and one-to-one tutorials and found the material works really well.

2 Introduction to Students
We suggest that you start by providing lots of questions or conversation openers on the whiteboard:
E.G.
• May I ask you a question?
• Do you have time to answer a question?
• I wish to ask a question, is that ok?

Discuss these with students and make sure they understand that they are asking permission to ask the question and that they will follow this up with a second question. Follow this up with what are commonly called WH questions:

• What...?
• When...?
• Why...?
• Where...? and
• How?

Make the point that you know 'How' is not a WH question but that it is an opening word for a question. All questions that start with these words are called 'open' questions. This means they cannot be answered with a simple 'yes' or 'no'. Questions that can be answered 'yes' or 'no' are closed questions.

Talk about these questions with the students and ask them to practise by asking each other these questions.

Ask the students to think up questions using the WH questions. They then need to ask another person in the class. When the students are comfortable with this, ask them to write down questions and write their answers.

Using the Media
A useful activity is to pre-record an interview off the radio. Look for the use of 'WH' questions in the interview. We have provided a transcript on the disc for you to use with your students. This is from a real interview by the journalist Andrew Marr with former British Prime Minister Sir John Major. Ask the students to highlight 'WH' questions.

Abraham Zapruder

On the site www.jfk.org/the-collections/...zapruder.../zapruder-interview-transcript/, you will find a transcript of a TV interview with Abraham Zapruder. Mr Zapruder was the man who filmed the murder of the US President John Kennedy in 1963 in Dallas, Texas.

Again ask the students to go through the interview looking for 'WH' questions.

You can see the interview here https://www.youtube.com/watch?v=JLqOGEBcjnl, You Tube.

Sir David Frost and Former President Richard Nixon

One of the most famous interviews took place when Frost interviewed Nixon. Nixon had 'stepped down' from office because of the Watergate Scandal. Here is an edited transcript http://www.theguardian.com/theguardian/2007/sep/07/greatinterviews1.

You may have to explain the Watergate Scandal to students. Try these sites:

www.thejournal.ie/what-was-watergate-14-facts-richard-nixon-494970-J...
www.scholastic.com/browse/article.jsp?id=11259,
www.scholastic.com/teachers/article/case-watergate

Esl Lounge Student

There is an excellent transcript of a supposed interview with an actress, you can find it here http://www.esl-lounge.com/student/listening/4L1-actress-transcript.php

My Favourite Film

There is a very nice listening skills practice transcript here, http://learnenglishteens.britishcouncil.org/sites/teens/files/my_favourite_film_-_transcript_1.pdf

This American Life from WBEZ has a very useful radio archive by date. You can find it here, http://www.thisamericanlife.org/radio-archives#2000

Serial: This is now a world famous podcast and is compulsive, you can find it here, https://serialpodcast.org/

Old Radio Show: You can download old radio shows, mostly American, here https://archive.org/details/oldtimeradio

These sites were available on the day we checked, they may not be available when you read this page.

Teachers may copy these pages for use in their own school. Rights are not transferable.

Activity One

1   What can you remember about going to school when you were a child?

2   What is the name of your favourite tv show?

3   Where did you last go on holiday?

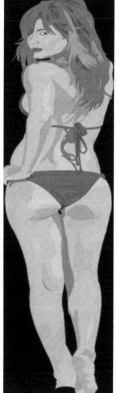

4 What did you do today?

5 Where do you live?

6 Who did you speak to today?

7 Do you wear a uniform at work?

8 What do you do for a living?

9 How long have you been working there?

Teachers may copy these pages for use in their own school. Rights are not transferable.

Activity One Continued

10 Do you like coffee or tea?

11 What is your favourite meal?

12 Do you like cooking?

13 What sports do you enjoy watching and playing?

14 Which tv channel has the best sport coverage?

15 Do you like watching women's sport?

16 What is you boss like?

17 What time do you start work in the morning?

18 Do you work a shift pattern?

19 How long have you worked there?

20 Do they make you feel welcome at work?

© 2016 Lawler Education
Teachers may copy these pages for use in their own school. Rights are not transferable.

What Do These Sayings Mean?

You'll be in hot water

You've put your foot in it

Hit the nail on the head

As light as a feather

Pulling my leg

A piece of cake

Raining cats and dogs

Smell a rat

Shake a leg

Once in a blue moon

Every Preston Guild

Nose to the grindstone

Name_____   Match the card with its meaning

A piece of cake	Wake and get up out of bed, not laze
Nose to the grindstone	Suspect something is wrong
Shake a leg	Work and focus on work for a long time
Smell a rat	An easy job

© 2016 Lawler Education
Teachers may copy these pages for use in their own school. Rights are not transferable.

This is an old Morgan car.

- Do you like this car?

- Would this car suit your family needs?

- Early versions of this car were popular with RAF officers in the Second World War, why do you think that was the case?

- Morgans are hand made cars, what does this mean?

- Do you think ordinary people could afford to buy a Morgan?

- These cars work with a stick shift, what does 'stick shift' mean?

Teachers may copy these pages for use in their own school. Rights are not transferable.

Tutor Notes

The purpose of this section is to increase student vocabulary.

We suggest that you start by asking students for details of activities they do at home, or at work or in the community.

- What items, resources or equipment do they need to complete these activities?
- Note down any new vocabulary words for later discussion.

If the students are struggling with these activities try:
- A photo as a stimulus,
- Ask them to describe their journey to work or college,

The point we are making is that to start a conversation, we need to use the 'WH' questions to get open responses.

For Example
Using this photograph (see the powerpoint display on the disc with this book)

What can you say about the person in the photograph?
- What gender is the person?
- How old do you think she is?
- What sort of mood is she in?
- Where do you think she is from?
- Where do you think she might be going?
- What might the headscarf indicate?

The whole purpose is to generate language and to use language purposefully.

Similarly by asking them for their journey to work or college they are having to recall and use purposeful language.

 © 2016 Lawler Education
Teachers may copy these pages for use in their own school. Rights are not transferable.

Name_____

To get ready to go to work, I need to:

_____

_____

_____

To do this I need to:

_____

_____

_____

Vocabulary: What do these words mean?

Get dressed _____

Shave_____

Clean teeth_____

Cook Breakfast_____

Shower_____

Teachers may copy these pages for use in their own school. Rights are not transferable.

Name_____

To paint a room, I need:

_____

_____

_____

How do I do this?_____

_____

_____

_____

Vocabulary: What do these words mean?

Ladder_____

Paint brush_____

Roller_____

Paint_____

Face goggles_____

14 © 2016 Lawler Education
Teachers may copy these pages for use in their own school. Rights are not transferable.

Name_____

1   What do I need to wash the dishes?

_____

_____

_____

2   How do I do this?

_____

_____

_____

_____

Vocabulary: What do these words mean?

plug_____

taps _____

rinse_____

tea towel_____

Teachers may copy these pages for use in their own school. Rights are not transferable.

Name_____

1 What do I need to do to pump petrol?

_____

_____

_____

2 How do I do this?

_____

_____

_____

_____

Vocabulary: What do these words mean?

Vehicle_____

Hose _____

Nozzle_____

Pay point_____

© 2016 Lawler Education
Teachers may copy these pages for use in their own school. Rights are not transferable.

Name_____

Draw arrows from the label to where you can see it on the page

microwave	kettle	washing up liquid

cooker	sink	toaster

© 2016 Lawler Education
Teachers may copy these pages for use in their own school. Rights are not transferable.

Name_____

Draw arrows from the label to where you can see it on the page

| holster | bin | screen wash bottles |

| credit card keypad | fuel pumped display | fuel company name |

 © 2016 Lawler Education
Teachers may copy these pages for use in their own school. Rights are not transferable.

Pick one of these topics and talk about it with your partner for one minute

Days of the week

Suggestions:
- Which days do you work on ?
- Which day is a holy day ?
- Which days do you go shopping ?

Months of the year

Suggestions:
- Which months are the U.K. winter ?
- Which month has Christmas ?
- Which days do you go shopping ?

News

Suggestions:
- Which tv news programmes do you watch?
- Which radio news do you listen to?
- What happened in the news yesterday?

Countries and Languages

Suggestions:
- Which languages do you speak?
- What countries have you visited?
- Where do you live now?

Common Places

Suggestions:
- Which bank do you use?
- Which doctor do you see?
- Where is the nearest post office?

© 2016 Lawler Education

Teachers may copy these pages for use in their own school. Rights are not transferable.

Teacher Notes

The purpose of this unit is for students to become more familiar with their city, town or location and increase their vocabulary. Students need a map of your locality.

Introduction to Students

We suggest that you ask straightforward questions like,
' What towns have you lived in ? '
' Can you write down your address and phone number ? '

On the white board flash up the Smart Board Activity Life Skills 1: Your Town. There are three versions of this activity, a slow version, a medium version and a fast version. Each activity is the same it is just the speed that is different
This is a set of anagrams. The students are against the clock. They use their fingers to move the balls into order to make the word. If they need to, they can press the clue to get some help to determine the word.

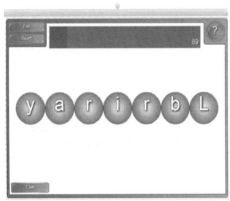

Method

After the introduction, use the My Town sheets to develop language regarding their area.
Places I go and *Where do my friends live ?* could be a home works.
Where do my friends live? needs professional judgement. Some people are rightly concerned about their contact details being in the public domain and some minority groups have issues with this matter. Therefore we suggest that you say to students, that if they are not happy giving their own address out, then put their name down care of the college

Feedback

This can be a fun discussion. You can discuss home locations, locations of the nearest supermarkets, schools, dr's surgeries/medical centres, primary/secondary schools, libraries, swimming pools, fast food restaurants

Now ask the students to write clear instructions in answer to the question, ' How do I get to (name of place) from (name of place). 'For example, ' To get from my home, to the doctor's, I walk down Catherine Street, turn right on the Melton Road and go up to Brown Street. The doctor's is on the corner.'

Take the students for a walk and ask them to record and narrate a video of their journey.

Teachers may copy these pages for use in their own school. Rights are not transferable.

They can then upload this to social media or link it through to the smart board and play their video to other students.

Be aware that not all students will be able to/ 'be allowed' to access social media so it is advisable to be cautious here. An alternative is to use Google maps for your area.

Going by Bus

Many people struggle with bus timetables, especially when English is not their first language. It is worth spending time with a timetable for your area and showing students how to plan a bus trip.

This is the site for Stage Coach, the bus company, https://www.stagecoachbus.com/timetables

We suggest you spend some time working with the 24 hour clock in English, to make this clear to students.

Safe Travel in Taxis

The vast majority of taxi drivers are decent honest people simply doing their job. Sadly some are not. It is therefore worth talking these issues through with students, especially female students who may be new to the country.

Make sure all students understand how to take photos on their phone and how to send them via their phone to a friend. This is a simple security measure that can be taken when a single woman gets into a cab. It is also worth telling them to keep a note of the company name from whom that taxi is booked and not just accept any man who arrives and says ' did someone book a taxi?'

For more on this, see The Crime Prevention Website, http://thecrimepreventionwebsite.com/safer-travel/809/safer-travel-in-taxis-and-cabs

Many students will now have a sat nav facility on their phone and may find this a useful tool. Alternatively there are online facilities like BBC Travel, or the AA or RAC where journeys can be planned. Finally for those who wish to 'do' Europe, they could consider Megabus.com which will give you and your students details of low cost travel in Europe.

© 2016 Lawler Education

Teachers may copy these pages for use in their own school. Rights are not transferable.

Name_____

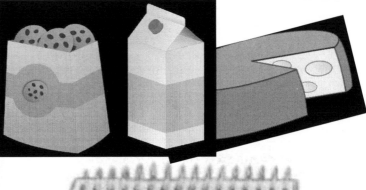

Think of several places you might want to go. Write down their names (e.g. supermarkets, fast food restaurants, movie theatre)

Find out where they are and mark them on your map. You may need to Google the name to get an address. List the ones you put on your map.

Teachers may copy these pages for use in their own school. Rights are not transferable.

Name_____

1 Find out where your friends or other students live and mark those places on your map.

2. Choose Four people and fill in their details.

Name_____

Address_____

_____

_____

Phone_____

Name_____

Address_____

_____

_____

Phone_____

Name_____

Address_____

_____

_____

Phone_____

Name_____

Address_____

_____

_____

Phone_____

I keep my friends contact details on my phone, It is really easy to do and means I can keep in touch.

© 2016 Lawler Education   23
Teachers may copy these pages for use in their own school. Rights are not transferable.

Teacher Notes

The purpose of this unit is to help students feel confident using the telephone.

Introduction

We suggest you discuss some basic etiquette with students.

For instance: When is it too early to ring?

When is it too late to ring?

What about Holy/Religious days, should these be respected as family time?

Preparing for the Phone Call

Talk through the purpose of the call with students.

Who are you calling? Family member? Friend? Professional e.g Doctor?

Why are you calling? To ask for information?
                      To impart information?

Do you have the phone number?

How can you find the number?   Phone Book? Online?

Finding the company website?

If necessary have the student write down the information they require before they make the call. This may make a stressful situation more manageable.

Make sure you encourage students to have a writing pad next to the phone and to write down the name of the person to whom they are talking. It is extremely easy to forget the name of the person with whom you are dealing.

 © 2016 Lawler Education
Teachers may copy these pages for use in their own school. Rights are not transferable.

The B.T. Website

The first thing is to google BT phone book, then open up the website. Then decide which tab to use and put the data in to search.

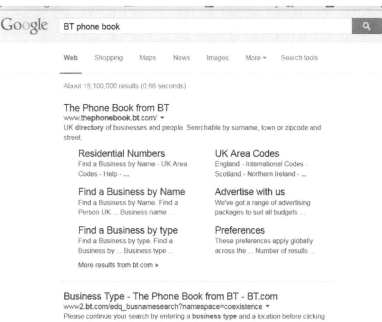

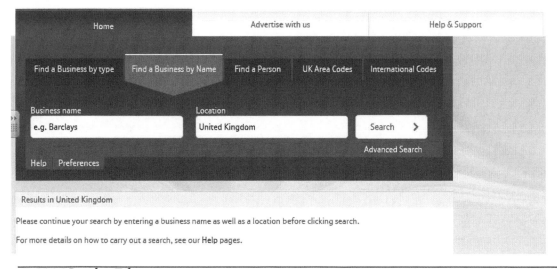

© 2016 Lawler Education   25
Teachers may copy these pages for use in their own school. Rights are not transferable.

Look up the names of some fellow students and see if they are listed in the phone book.

Remember, some people are Ex-Directory. This means they keep their number private and it is not listed in the phone book.

Use the website to find:

- The names of three plumbers in your area.
- The names of three electricians in your area.
- The phone number for the secondary school in your area.
- The details for your doctor.
- The details for your local hospital.
- The location and details of your library.
- The details for your local Post Office.

Build these into your contact list on your phone. We have edited the names on our contact details to keep their privacy.

Privacy is important, it is bad manners to pass on someone's details without their permission.

This does not apply to businesses who are usually very pleased to have their details spread to other people.

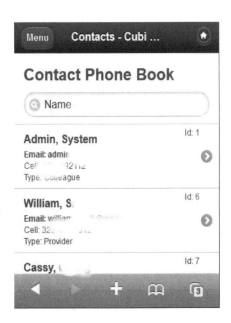

 © 2016 Lawler Education
Teachers may copy these pages for use in their own school. Rights are not transferable.

To find your local post office you can again use Google. You will then find the branch finder useful to find the local post office in your area.

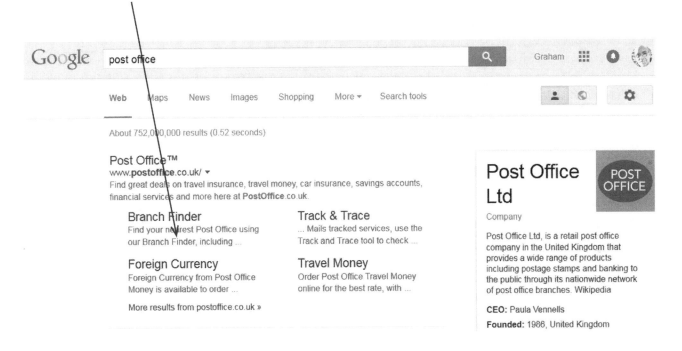

Open the website and click on the mail tab and you will find this:

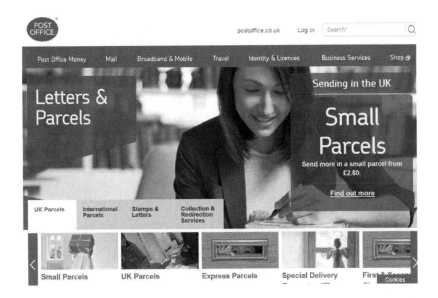

With a partner explore this site to find out how much it costs to send a 100g, 240mm by 165mm by 5mm maximum letter.

© 2016 Lawler Education
Teachers may copy these pages for use in their own school. Rights are not transferable.

Name_____

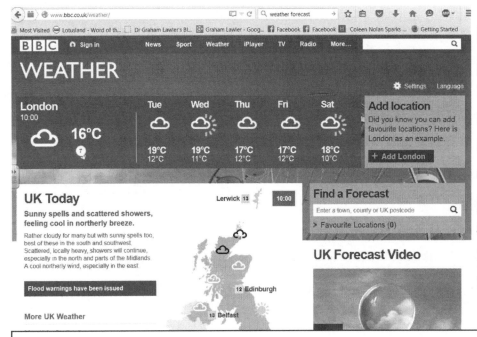

Using a smart-phone, Google the BBC weather report. On the right hand side you can put your area post code into the search engine and find the forecast for today.

Making a Doctor's Appointment

What information do you need to find out before you make the call?

What questions do you need to ask?

Use your Smartphone to find a local takeaway
Look for their phone number and write it here _____

How much is a meal for one? _____

Do they do family meals?   _____

Teachers may copy these pages for use in their own school. Rights are not transferable.

Name_____

Your teacher will play you an audio story, listen carefully to the story and use the words at the bottom of the page to fill in the gaps.

The day started fine, or so she thought. It was only when she was on the landing at _____that she realised something was wrong. She realised her feet were wet. Oh no, there was a leak some-where. She screamed for her _____, 'Philip'. He stumbled out of their bedroom after her and looked around. ' Where ? ' He was looking for the _____. She pointed down, ' Oh for goodness sake', he said.

That was when they saw it, the _____ was coming from the bath-room, it was _____under the bathroom door. She slowly opened the bathroom door, quite honestly fearful of what she would see. The bath was _____and the water was still running out of the tap. She turned the tap off. Someone in their house had taken a bath, put the plug in and left the taps _____and flooded the entire landing. The water was now running down the ____. She looked at Philip and he shook his head, they both looked at their daughter's bedroom door.
'Sweetie' said Philip, 'you up yet?'.
The door opened and their _____ walked out, she said
' my _____ are wet, oh I didn't...'

water   stairs teenager   overflowing   husband

home   danger   running   feet   seeping

© 2016 Lawler Education   29
Teachers may copy these pages for use in their own school. Rights are not transferable.

What is 'small talk'?   Name_____

Small talk is something that everyone does. It is chatter that some say is for no reason. Other people say it is an 'ice-breaker'. This means it is a way of getting to know someone.

Small talk is also known as...

Chewing the fat		Discussing the weather	
	Chatter		Natter

1. What are some subjects that could be small talk? Small talk is often the start of a conversation and usually isn't personal. You would also use small talk with someone you don't know very well.

_____   _____

_____   _____

_____   _____

2. Write down YES if you think that the subject IS small talk and NO if you think the subject is NOT small talk:

• the weather _____   • how much money you have _____

• a car accident you had ___   • sport ____

• what time you go to bed ___   • finding a job _____

• your problems _____   • your family ____

Teachers may copy these pages for use in their own school. Rights are not transferable.

Name_____

3. Make a list of four things you could talk about with somebody you have just met.

_____   _____

_____   _____

4. Make a list of four things you would not talk about with somebody you have just met.

_____   _____

_____   _____

5 Have you ever overheard people using small talk?

What was it about?

_____

_____

_____

_____

6. How could you use small talk to start a conversation?

What topics could you discuss that are non-threatening?

_____

_____

© 2016 Lawler Education   31
Teachers may copy these pages for use in their own school. Rights are not transferable.

Name_____

Let's Try It!

1. Choose a subject for small talk and write down a few questions and comments about that subject.

For example: WEATHER

- Do you think it was warm today?

- It's been wet again!

- It has been very windy lately.

- Today it was very close.

Think of two questions and two comments to do with a small talk subject and write them down.

Subject: _____

Question 1: _____

Comment 1: _____

Question 2: _____

Comment 2: _____

2. Find a partner and start talking small talk with them. Don't forget to talk as well as listen. Ask questions as well as answer them.

Teachers may copy these pages for use in their own school. Rights are not transferable.

3. When you start a small talk, it nearly always will develop into a proper conversation. Look at this: My girlfriend and I saw her friend Janish in town. She introduced me to her friend:

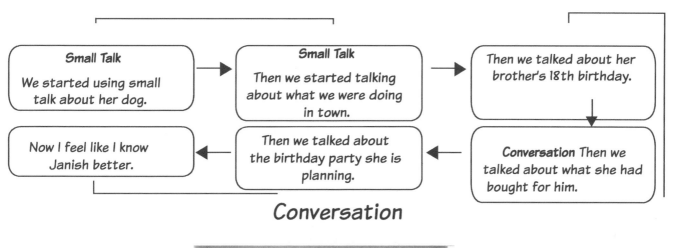

| Small Talk
We started using small talk about her dog. | → | Small Talk
Then we started talking about what we were doing in town. | → | Then we talked about her brother's 18th birthday. |
| Now I feel like I know Janish better. | ← | Then we talked about the birthday party she is planning. | ← | Conversation Then we talked about what she had bought for him. |

Conversation

4. Choose another partner and try your small talk again. What else did you start talking about?

Do you know how you started talking about that?

Do you know when it changed from small talk to a conversation? Write down here what else you talked about:

_____

_____

_____

_____

Teachers may copy these pages for use in their own school. Rights are not transferable.

Tutor Notes

1.   The purpose of this unit is to help students learn more about the possessions in their own home.

2.   We recommend that when you are introducing this to students that you initiate a conversation on naming items, and describing their purpose, that they can find in their own home.

3.   If you have students from other countries who have come to the U.K., you may find there are cultural differences. For instance, one of our students is from a family from Poland. They have moved into a home and developed the home by fitting new external doors that open outwards. This is in keeping with the manner in which doors open in other European countries open outwards. British doors traditionally open inwards. The student pointed out that when the traditional British door is opened inwards, if it has been raining it takes the rain inside. There is a certain logic in this approach. Similarly differences in cooking styles can lead to great discussions.

4.   We found that some students found it reassuring to name the product in their home language and then again in English. The argument in favour of this is that they are learning two words for everything. There is evidence from Wales that bilingual students actually learn more efficiently because they have two languages.

5.   Continuing the activity, we suggest that you periodically stop the activity and ask a quick quiz, say six questions , about the household item. If they are not sure of the name of the item then do prompt them and if needed, give them the name but do ask them how to spell it.   We also suggest that you occasionally track back in the lesson and point to previous items asking, ' what was this called again?' and ' How do I spell the name of this item?'

6.   Ask the students to match an item with its use. Try playing 20 questions based on household items or try a memory game in the style of the Generation Game. This link will take you to a 1974 edition of the Bruce Forsyth game show, https://www.youtube.com/watch?v=f5aYT9iBml8

Teachers may copy these pages for use in their own school. Rights are not transferable.

Name_____

These are_____

You buy them at _____

They are used for_____

These are_____

You buy them at _____

They are used for_____

These are_____

You buy them at _____

They are used for_____

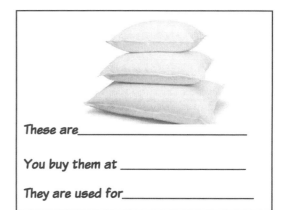

These are_____

You buy them at _____

They are used for_____

These are_____

You buy them at _____

They are used for_____

These are_____

You buy them at _____

They are used for_____

These are_____

You buy them at _____

They are used for_____

These are_____

You buy them at _____

They are used for_____

Teachers may copy these pages for use in their own school. Rights are not transferable.

Name_____

Take this list home. Tick each item you find. Write the room where you find it.

slippers ◯	wall decorations ◯	settee ◯	fridge ◯
oven ◯	DIY Tools ◯	Car Keys ◯	coffee ◯
cushions ◯	duvet ◯	curtains ◯	desk ◯
telephone ◯	kettle ◯	mug ◯	tv ◯
shower ◯	cutlery ◯	photograph ◯	computer ◯

Take this to your workplace or college/school/academy.
Write down the place where you find these things.

pen ◯	filing cabinet ◯	telephone ◯
desk ◯	table ◯	desk lamp ◯
kettle ◯	cardboard box ◯	in trays ◯
frdige ◯	time sheet ◯	notice boards ◯
laptop ◯	reception desk ◯	white boards ◯
fridge ◯	printer ◯	coffee machine ◯
photocopier ◯	tea ◯	heater ◯

 © 2016 Lawler Education
Teachers may copy these pages for use in their own school. Rights are not transferable.

Name_____ match the labels with the images

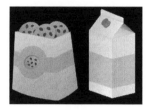

yoghurt

apple

tin of beans

milk and biscuits

cup of tea

© 2016 Lawler Education
Teachers may copy these pages for use in their own school. Rights are not transferable.

Tutor's Notes

The purpose of this section is to help students be more comfortable with conversations.

Introduction to students

We suggest you recap asking questions and small talk. It is important that students understand how conversation with people is a good way to improve both their listening and questioning skills.

Open Questions

Revisit the mock radio interviews we completed earlier. This will re-affirm open questioning.

The 'Yes/No' Game

The traditional 'yes/NO' game was a game show favourite. The original game asked contestants closed questions and they had to try and avoid saying either yes or no. This is a great way of developing language skills and is also a lot of fun. The skill for you as a teacher, in this game, is to ask closed questions. The students need answer without saying 'yes' or 'no'.

On the day we checked there was a yes/No game on this site,
http://yesnogame.thebigchallenge.com

There is also a card game called the Yes/No game that you may wish to acquire, this link will show you the game:
http://www.amazon.co.uk/THE-YES-NO-GAME-FAMILY/dp/B00GTXWAD2

Teachers may copy these pages for use in their own school. Rights are not transferable.

Name_____

1. You are making a phone call to ask for information, write 2 questions, that start with 'how', you could ask here.

2. Start a conversation by asking 2 'how' questions, write the questions here.

© 2016 Lawler Education
Teachers may copy these pages for use in their own school. Rights are not transferable.

Name_____

1. Starting conversations with a 'Wh' questions is a good way to find out information. Write 2 questions starting with 'where' here.

 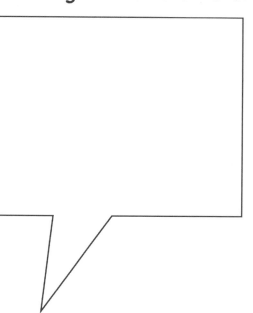

2. Start a conversation by asking 2 ' Wh' questions. Write your questions here.

 © 2016 Lawler Education
Teachers may copy these pages for use in their own school. Rights are not transferable.

'Vox pop' means ' Voice of the People'. This is the type of broadcasting package where people on radio or tv ask one question and then edit the answers together.

Ask students to use their phones to interview each other. Most phones have a voice recorder. They then need to download the answers from their phones to a computer and edit the material. If you do not have an editor then try downloading Audacity, this is a free software package and can be downloaded from here:

http://audacityteam.org/

You will probably need to ask for technician help and permission to download the software.

You can have some fun with this activity. For example, if the students start by asking, ' who is the Prime Minister?' This then will elicit the response of the present day incumbent. Then they could change the question but later edit out that question. If the second question is for example, ' Who is the breakfast show dj on BBC Radio One?', the format will then be:

'Who is the Prime Minister?'
Answers 1, 2 and 3 will all state the present day incumbent
Now change the question to
' Who is the breakfast show dj on BBC Radio One?
this will lead to a different answer, i.e. the name of a disc jockey.

Now think of the outcome, there will only be one question at the start of the vox pop, have fun!

Teachers may copy these pages for use in their own school. Rights are not transferable.

Tutor Notes

The purpose of this unit is to provide students with effective strategies for communicating their problems.

When introducing this subject, we do advise caution. Students need to respect privacy and cultural beliefs are of vital importance.

The purpose of this activity is to help students formulate topics to discuss.

Students who are from other countries may not be use to the 'subtlety' of statements in English. They may need to be made aware of the underlying meaning of 'polite' style questions.

For example; ' I wonder if I may have...' is the polite way in English to say ' I want...'.

Similarly, ' I'm awfully sorry to disturb you but I wonder if I might...' is simply a polite way of saying ' Pay attention to me...'
This is often a surprise to people who are learning English.

Professional Judgement
In the same manner students need to understand that despite the cultural values of the country from which they may have come, in the U.K. equality is enshrined in law. We do know of situations where men have complained when women are in the room. In these circumstances it is vital, in our view, that the woman or women concerned are reassured that their rights are and will be respected.

Similarly students need to be aware that being assertive is not the same as being aggressive. You need to create scenarios where they can be assertive BUT not become aggressive despite how much provocation the student receives. In the event of a suspected physical attack or an actual attack, students need to know how to contact the police for support and what to say to the police

If this is an issue with your students, ensure the female students are aware that there are ' places of safety' should they need them. One website to make them aware of is:
http://www.refuge.org.uk/what-we-do/our-services/refuges/

As we have said elsewhere, we cannot guarantee this site will be there when you need it. Therefore it is also worth ensuring that students know how to Google information.

Teachers may copy these pages for use in their own school. Rights are not transferable.

Set up your own *Question Time* panel. You may need to explain to students that *Question Time* is a current affairs programme on BBC TV.

Professional Judgement
It may be the case that students who have come from elsewhere have endured trauma and therefore professional judgement is needed here, as to the appropriateness of this activity. It is important that all students are briefed to stick to policy arguments and not to indulge in personal attacks in order that self-esteem is intact for all involved.

Set up the panel
Set up a panel in the manner of the *Question Time* tv programme.
You will need a chairperson and then panel delegates. The tv programme has 5 delegates and the chair person.
The better approach is to have students in the panel who represent all political views.

Programme format
Ask all audience members to write the same question on two cards, one card must also have their name on it. Then the chairperson should chose the questions at random and ask each member of the panel to address the audience. Don't forget to allow audience participation, the objective here is to encourage conversation.

As a follow up encourage students to view the tv programme or similar political programmes.

Teachers may copy these pages for use in their own school. Rights are not transferable.

£20 Lawler Education Voucher for detailed and complete reviews. The purpose of this form is to give you, the teacher, an opportunity for improvement/positive feedback.

Resource Name_____ Resource ISBN_____

Your Name_____ Your Position _____

School Name_____

Address _____

_____

Overall, what do you think about this resource ? _____

_____

_____

How does it help your students ?_____

_____

_____

What could you say to a colleague in a neighbouring school to persuade them to use this resource ?

_____

_____

How well does it match the specification and which specification is it ? _____

_____

Other Comments, suggestions for improvement, errors, please give the page number

_____

Resources I would like published

Resources I might like to write, or have written, for consideration for publishing.

Fax: 01745 826606 email: info@graham-lawler.com
post: Lawler Education, Lamorna House, Abergele LL22 8DD

44 © 2016 Lawler Education
Teachers may copy these pages for use in their own school. Rights are not transferable.